My First Year
IN RECOVERY

A Journal for the Journey

*"To live a life in recovery is to live in freedom
from the slavery of addiction and in a full, rich,
rewarding way that has meaning and value."*

RECOVERY A TO Z: A HANDBOOK OF TWELVE-STEP
KEY TERMS AND PHRASES

CENTRAL RECOVERY PRESS

LAS VEGAS, NEVADA

To those who have yet to find recovery

CENTRAL RECOVERY PRESS

CENTRAL RECOVERY PRESS
Central Recovery Press (CRP) is committed to publishing exceptional material addressing addiction treatment, recovery, and behavioral health care, including original and quality books, audio/visual communications, and Web-based new media. Through a diverse selection of titles, it seeks to impact the behavioral health care field with a broad range of unique resources for professionals, recovering individuals, and their families. For more information, visit www.centralrecoverypress.com.

Central Recovery Press, Las Vegas, NV 89129
© 2008, 2010 by Central Recovery Press

ISBN-13: 978-1-949481-50-1

Publisher: Central Recovery Press
              3371 N Buffalo Drive
              Las Vegas, NV 89129

Cover design and interior by Sara Streifel, Think Creative Design

❧ Your Journey Begins ❧

My first year clean was full of magical changes. I had so many learning experiences
I couldn't even begin to remember them all. I had a calendar I marked every day
clean on, and I carefully circled each milestone. I also kept a journal my first year
clean that I did on my own, but it had no focus other than my random thoughts.

Looking back, I thought, "Wouldn't it be nice to have a detailed and instructive
guide where I could have listed the people who helped me, my first meeting list, my
sponsor, and other important people and events? Wouldn't it be nice to have written
about the awakening I had and about all those special moments?"

So much happens in our first year that it is impossible to remember it all.
I wish today I had something more to look back on and relive those experiences—
the good and the bad. What a wonderful tool to measure my growth and
to stay in gratitude for where I came from and how far I have come today.

I hope you enjoy this journal—created by individuals in recovery, for individuals
in recovery, and based upon the things we wished we had in our first year. As with
recovery, I truly believe you will get out of it as much as you put in.

Best wishes to you as you embark upon your own journey of recovery.

FRANK, IN RECOVERY FOR TWENTY-TWO YEARS

My journey begins today.

Today's Date _____   Today is my FIRST day in recovery.

Today I *met* _____

_____

_____

_____

_____

I *feel* _____

_____

_____

_____

_____

_____

_____

_____

_____

_____

_____

_____

_____

"EVERYONE WHO GOT WHERE HE IS HAD TO BEGIN WHERE HE WAS."
ROBERT LOUIS STEVENSON (1850–1894)

Today's Date _____   Days in Recovery_____

When I *dream* of my future, I see _____

_____

_____

_____

_____

At *my* first twelve–step meeting, I felt_____

_____

_____

_____

_____

_____

_____

_____

_____

_____

_____

_____

_____

_____

"MY FEELINGS AT MY FIRST MEETING WERE OVERWHELMING FEAR AND PANIC,
BUT ALSO A SMALL BIT OF HOPE."

FRANK, IN RECOVERY FOR TWENTY-TWO YEARS

Today's Date _____   Days in Recovery _____

I am *grateful* for _____

_____

_____

_____

_____

In order to reach my *dreams,* I need to _____

_____

_____

_____

_____

_____

_____

_____

_____

_____

_____

_____

_____

_____

_____

"FOCUSING ON THE THINGS I CAN BE GRATEFUL FOR OR WRITING A GRATITUDE LIST
HELPED ME A LOT DURING MY FIRST YEAR."

TRAVIS, IN RECOVERY FOR SIX YEARS

Today's Date _____   Days in Recovery_____

My biggest *accomplishment* today was _____

_____

_____

_____

_____

The fog is starting to *clear* and now I am worried _____

_____

_____

_____

_____

_____

_____

_____

_____

_____

_____

_____

_____

_____

_____

"I'LL WORRY ABOUT THAT IF AND WHEN IT HAPPENS—AND NOT BEFORE!"
SYDNEY (1925–2005), IN RECOVERY FOR THIRTY YEARS

Today's Date _____   Days in Recovery _____

To help me stay in recovery, I _____

_____

_____

_____

_____

The most helpful thing I *learned* at my most recent twelve-step meeting was_____

_____

_____

_____

_____

_____

_____

_____

_____

_____

_____

_____

_____

_____

"ONE OF THE FIRST PRINCIPLES MANY ADDICTS LEARN WHEN THEY
START THEIR RECOVERY JOURNEY IS RESPONSIBILITY."

TAILS OF RECOVERY: ADDICTS AND THE PETS THAT LOVE THEM

Today's Date _____   Days in Recovery _____

Today I was *successful* at _____

_____

_____

_____

_____

I *hope* for _____

_____

_____

_____

_____

_____

_____

_____

_____

Today I learned	Today I did something positive for my recovery by
_____	_____
_____	_____
_____	_____
_____	_____
_____	_____

Today's Date _____   Days in Recovery _____

Today I feel *safest* at_____

_____

_____

_____

_____

To keep my life from becoming *unmanageable* again, I know I must _____

_____

_____

_____

_____

_____

_____

_____

_____

_____

_____

_____

_____

_____

_____

"AT MY FIRST MEETING I FELT SAFE AND UNDERSTOOD."
BOBBY, (1934-2008) IN RECOVERY FOR THIRTY-FOUR YEARS

Today's Date _____   Days in Recovery _____

Today I *met* _____

_____

_____

_____

_____

I would like a *sponsor* who _____

_____

_____

_____

_____

_____

_____

_____

_____

_____

_____

_____

_____

_____

❖━━❖❖━━❖

"I CHOSE MY FIRST SPONSOR BECAUSE SHE HAD A GENTLE SPIRIT.
I STRUGGLED SO LONG WITH SELF-HATRED THAT I NEEDED SOMEONE LOVING
AND GENTLE, ESPECIALLY SINCE I COULD NOT BE THAT WAY WITH MYSELF.
SHE HAD SOLID RECOVERY, AND I WANTED WHAT SHE HAD."

NANCY, IN RECOVERY FOR TWENTY-SEVEN YEARS

Today's Date _____ Days in Recovery _____

My biggest *challenge* today was _____

_____

_____

_____

_____

I met this *challenge* by _____

_____

_____

_____

_____

_____

_____

_____

_____

_____

_____

_____

_____

_____

_____

"GREAT WORKS ARE PERFORMED NOT BY STRENGTH, BUT BY PERSEVERANCE."

SAMUEL JOHNSON (1709–1784)

Today's Date _____   Days in Recovery _____

Today I *hope* _____

_____

_____

_____

_____

When I think about *surrender*, I believe _____

_____

_____

_____

_____

_____

_____

_____

_____

_____

_____

_____

_____

_____

_____

"THE GREATNESS OF A MAN'S POWER IS THE MEASURE OF HIS SURRENDER."
WILLIAM BOOTH (1829–1912)

Today's Date _____ Days in Recovery _____

I am taking care of myself *emotionally* by _____

_____

_____

_____

_____

I am taking care of myself *spiritually* by _____

_____

_____

_____

_____

_____

_____

_____

_____

_____

_____

_____

_____

_____

"TO ACCOMPLISH GREAT THINGS, WE MUST DREAM AS WELL AS ACT."

ANATOLE FRANCE (1844–1924)

Today's Date _____   Days in Recovery _____

The best *suggestion* I've heard so far is _____

_____

_____

_____

_____

Today I am *grateful* for _____

_____

_____

_____

_____

_____

_____

_____

Today I learned	Today I did something positive for my recovery by
_____	_____
_____	_____
_____	_____
_____	_____
_____	_____

Today's Date _____   Days in Recovery _____

To describe my experience of this *disease* to someone else, I say _____

_____

_____

_____

_____

I enjoy being in *recovery* because _____

_____

_____

_____

_____

_____

_____

_____

_____

_____

_____

_____

_____

_____

_____

"HEALTH IS A STATE OF COMPLETE PHYSICAL, MENTAL, AND SOCIAL WELL-BEING
AND NOT MERELY THE ABSENCE OF DISEASE OR INFIRMITY."
PREAMBLE TO THE CONSTITUTION OF THE WORLD HEALTH ORGANIZATION *

Today's Date _____ Days in Recovery_____

Today I *learned* _____

_____

_____

_____

_____

The step I am currently writing on is *teaching* me _____

_____

_____

_____

_____

_____

_____

_____

_____

_____

_____

_____

_____

_____

❖

"THOSE WHO EMBRACE THE PRINCIPLES FOUND IN THE TWELVE STEPS
LEARN TO LIVE A LIFE FILLED WITH DIGNITY, ACCEPTANCE, COMPASSION, AND TRUST."

TAILS OF RECOVERY: ADDICTS AND THE PETS THAT LOVE THEM

Today's Date _____   Days in Recovery _____

The most *important* thing to me today is _____

_____

_____

_____

_____

_____

I envision my *higher power* to be _____

_____

_____

_____

_____

_____

_____

_____

_____

_____

_____

_____

_____

_____

"AN ENCHANTED WORLD IS ONE THAT SPEAKS TO THE SOUL, TO THE
MYSTERIOUS DEPTHS OF THE HEART AND IMAGINATION WHERE WE FIND
VALUE, LOVE, AND UNION WITH THE WORLD AROUND US."
SIR THOMAS MORE (1478–1535)

Today's Date _____   Days in Recovery_____

I *connected* with my higher power today by _____

_____

_____

_____

_____

Today my *dreams* are _____

_____

_____

_____

_____

_____

_____

_____

_____

_____

_____

_____

_____

_____

_____

"WHATEVER YOU CAN DO OR DREAM YOU CAN BEGIN IT.
BOLDNESS HAS GENIUS, POWER, AND MAGIC IN IT."
JOHANN WOLFGANG VON GOETHE (1749–1832)

Today's Date _____   Days in Recovery_____

The best *slogan* I heard at a meeting is_____

_____

_____

_____

_____

I am *participating* in the fellowship by _____

_____

_____

_____

_____

_____

_____

_____

_____

_____

_____

_____

_____

—————————————————————————◆❖◆—————————————————————————

"MY BIGGEST FEAR IN MY FIRST YEAR WAS THAT THE TWELVE-STEP PROGRAM I ATTEND
WOULDN'T WORK FOR ME BECAUSE NOTHING I EVER TRIED HAD WORKED UP TO THAT POINT.
I WAS WRONG. I WORKED IT, AND IT WORKED FOR ME."
FRANK, IN RECOVERY FOR TWENTY-TWO YEARS

Today's Date _____   Days in Recovery _____

Today I was of *service* to _____

_____

_____

_____

_____

I feel *strongest* when I _____

_____

_____

_____

_____

_____

_____

_____

_____

Today I learned	Today I did something positive for my recovery by
_____	_____
_____	_____
_____	_____
_____	_____
_____	_____

Today's Date _____   Days in Recovery _____

Today was *different* because _____

_____

_____

_____

_____

Today I *tried* _____

_____

_____

_____

_____

_____

_____

_____

_____

_____

_____

_____

_____

"NO MAN KNOWS WHAT HE CAN DO UNTIL HE TRIES."
PUBLILIUS SYRUS (85–43 BC)

Today's Date _____   Days in Recovery _____

Today I *reached out* to _____

_____

_____

_____

_____

I want to stay in recovery because _____

_____

_____

_____

_____

_____

_____

_____

_____

_____

_____

_____

_____

_____

"THE ADMISSION OF POWERLESSNESS PAVES THE WAY FOR A REALISTIC OPINION
OF THE SELF AND LAYS THE FOUNDATION OF ALL THE OTHER STEPS."

RECOVERY A TO Z: A HANDBOOK OF TWELVE-STEP KEY TERMS AND PHRASES

Today's Date _____   Days in Recovery _____

Today I *feel* _____

_____

_____

_____

_____

In order to *stay* in recovery, I need _____

_____

_____

_____

_____

_____

_____

_____

_____

_____

_____

_____

_____

"TO PERSEVERE, TRUSTING IN WHAT HOPES HE HAS, IS COURAGE IN A MAN."
EURIPIDES (480–406 BC)

Today's Date _____   Days in Recovery _____

Right now, *sanity* means the following to me _____

_____

_____

_____

_____

Today I understand *insanity* to be _____

_____

_____

_____

_____

_____

_____

_____

_____

_____

_____

_____

_____

"IF YOU WANT TO HEAR INSANITY,
JUST ASK ADDICTS WHY THEY ARE OR AREN'T DOING SOMETHING!"
SYDNEY (1925–2005), IN RECOVERY FOR THIRTY YEARS

Today's Date _____ Days in Recovery _____

Today I am *writing* on Step _____

_____

_____

_____

_____

Some of the *principles* I am learning are _____

_____

_____

_____

_____

_____

_____

_____

_____

_____

_____

_____

_____

_____

"ALL WRITING IS USELESS THAT DOES NOT PROVIDE A STIMULUS TO ACTIVITY."

FRIEDRICH NIETZSCHE (1844–1900)

Today's Date _____   Days in Recovery _____

Today I had an *opportunity* to _____

_____

_____

_____

_____

From that opportunity, I *learned* _____

_____

_____

_____

_____

_____

_____

_____

_____

Today I learned	Today I did something positive for my recovery by
_____	_____
_____	_____
_____	_____
_____	_____
_____	_____

Today's Date _____   Days in Recovery _____

Today I am *going* to _____

_____

_____

_____

_____

Today I finally *did* _____

_____

_____

_____

_____

_____

_____

_____

_____

_____

_____

_____

_____

_____

"THE MAN WHO SAYS IT CANNOT BE DONE
SHOULD NOT INTERRUPT THE MAN WHO IS DOING."
CHINESE PROVERB

Today's Date _____   Days in Recovery _____

When I think about my *willingness,* I believe _____

_____

_____

_____

_____

The person I most *admire* right now is _____

_____

_____

_____

_____

_____

_____

_____

_____

_____

_____

_____

_____

—◆❖◆—

"THE THIRTY- AND SIXTY-DAY CHIPS MEANT A LOT TO ME.
I COULDN'T FATHOM STAYING CLEAN FOR YEARS WHEN I CAME INTO RECOVERY,
BUT THIRTY DAYS WAS POSSIBLE. THE CHIPS WERE SOMETHING I COULD
LOOK FORWARD TO—A CHALLENGE I BELIEVED I COULD ATTAIN."
TRAVIS, IN RECOVERY FOR SIX YEARS

Today's Date _____   Days in Recovery _____

Today I *learned* _____

_____

_____

_____

_____

I *believe* I am _____

_____

_____

_____

_____

_____

_____

_____

_____

_____

_____

_____

_____

_____

"BAD TIMES HAVE A SCIENTIFIC VALUE....
WE LEARN GEOLOGY THE MORNING AFTER THE EARTHQUAKE."
RALPH WALDO EMERSON (1803–1882)

Today's Date _____   Days in Recovery _____

Today I *want* to _____

_____

_____

_____

_____

Today, being in *recovery* means _____

_____

_____

_____

_____

_____

_____

_____

_____

_____

_____

_____

_____

_____

❖

"I HAVE ALSO LEARNED FROM EXPERIENCE THAT
THE GREATER PART OF OUR HAPPINESS OR MISERY DEPENDS UPON
OUR DISPOSITIONS AND NOT UPON OUR CIRCUMSTANCES."
MARTHA WASHINGTON (1731–1802)

Today's Date _____   Days in Recovery _____

I find *hope* and *courage* in _____

_____

_____

_____

_____

From my sponsor I am *learning* _____

_____

_____

_____

_____

_____

_____

_____

_____

_____

_____

_____

_____

"FOR STRENGTH, COURAGE, AND HOPE,
I LEAN ON MY SPONSOR AND HIGHER POWER."
BOBBY, (1934-2008) IN RECOVERY FOR THIRTY-FOUR YEARS

Today's Date _____   Days in Recovery _____

Today I *hope* to _____

_____

_____

_____

_____

I think I am making *progress* when I look at _____

_____

_____

_____

_____

_____

_____

_____

_____

Today I learned	Today I did something positive for my recovery by
_____	_____
_____	_____
_____	_____
_____	_____

Today's Date _____ Days in Recovery _____

The step I am currently writing on is *helping* me to_____

_____

_____

_____

_____

I am beginning to *feel* better about _____

_____

_____

_____

_____

_____

_____

_____

_____

_____

_____

_____

_____

_____

_____

"ONE WORD OR A PLEASING SMILE IS OFTEN ENOUGH
TO RAISE UP A SADDENED AND WOUNDED SOUL."
ST. THERESE DE LISIEUX (1873–1897)

Today's Date _____   Days in Recovery _____

The things I find most *surprising* about recovery are _____

_____

_____

_____

_____

Today I am *grateful* for _____

_____

_____

_____

_____

_____

_____

_____

_____

_____

_____

_____

_____

_____

_____

"TWO MEN LOOK OUT THE SAME PRISON BARS:
ONE SEES MUD AND THE OTHER STARS."
FREDERICK LANGBRIDGE (1849–1923)

Today's Date _____   Days in Recovery _____

Today I was *challenged* by_____

_____

_____

_____

_____

This challenge helped me to *understand* _____

_____

_____

_____

_____

_____

_____

_____

_____

_____

_____

_____

_____

"THE GEM CANNOT BE POLISHED WITHOUT FRICTION,
NOR MAN PERFECTED WITHOUT TRIALS."
CHINESE PROVERB

Today's Date _____   Days in Recovery _____

Today I *learned* the following about myself _____

_____

_____

_____

_____

When I think about where I am in my life right now, I *believe* _____

_____

_____

_____

_____

_____

_____

_____

_____

_____

_____

_____

_____

_____

_____

"FOR A MAN TO CONQUER HIMSELF
IS THE FIRST AND NOBLEST OF ALL VICTORIES."
PLATO (428–348 BC)

Today's Date _____   Days in Recovery _____

Today I understand *truth* to be _____

_____

_____

_____

_____

In reaching out to others, I am *learning* _____

_____

_____

_____

_____

_____

_____

_____

_____

_____

_____

_____

_____

_____

"TRUTH IS THE ONLY SAFE GROUND TO STAND ON."
ELIZABETH CADY STANTON (1815–1902)

Today's Date _____   Days in Recovery _____

Today my sponsor *helped* me the most by_____

_____

_____

_____

_____

When I talk to my *higher power,* I focus on _____

_____

_____

_____

_____

_____

_____

_____

_____

Today I learned	Today I did something positive for my recovery by
_____	_____
_____	_____
_____	_____
_____	_____
_____	_____

Today's Date _____   Days in Recovery _____

The things I have *changed* so far are _____

_____

_____

_____

_____

I *feel* _____

_____

_____

_____

_____

_____

_____

_____

_____

_____

_____

_____

_____

_____

"CHANGE IS NOT MADE WITHOUT INCONVENIENCE,
EVEN FROM WORSE TO BETTER."
RICHARD HOOKER (1554–1600)

Today's Date _____   Days in Recovery _____

The *hardest* things about recovery right now are _____

_____

_____

_____

_____

The *best* things about recovery right now are _____

_____

_____

_____

_____

_____

_____

_____

_____

_____

_____

_____

_____

_____

_____

"FAITH IS THE SUBSTANCE OF THINGS HOPED FOR,
THE EVIDENCE OF THINGS NOT SEEN."
BIBLE: NEW TESTAMENT, HEBREWS 11:1

Today's Date _____ Days in Recovery _____

The *connection* between my higher power and my recovery is _____

_____

_____

_____

_____

Recovery is helping me to _____

_____

_____

_____

_____

_____

_____

_____

_____

_____

_____

_____

_____

_____

"TWO THINGS FILL THE MIND WITH EVER NEW AND INCREASING WONDER AND AWE,
THE MORE OFTEN AND THE MORE SERIOUSLY REFLECTION CONCENTRATES
UPON THEM: THE STARRY HEAVEN ABOVE ME AND THE MORAL LAW WITHIN ME."
IMMANUEL KANT (1724–1804)

Today's Date _____   Days in Recovery _____

The four words I use to *describe* me at this moment are _____

_____

_____

_____

_____

As I *write* in this journal, I am learning _____

_____

_____

_____

_____

_____

_____

_____

_____

_____

_____

_____

_____

_____

"YOU CANNOT PREVENT THE BIRDS OF SORROW FROM FLYING OVER YOUR HEAD,
BUT YOU CAN PREVENT THEM FROM BUILDING NESTS IN YOUR HAIR."

CHINESE PROVERB

Today's Date _____   Days in Recovery_____

I am learning to face my *fears* today by _____

_____

_____

_____

_____

As I *face* my fears, I feel _____

_____

_____

_____

_____

_____

_____

_____

_____

_____

_____

_____

"MY BIGGEST FEARS REVOLVED AROUND MY NUMEROUS FAILED ATTEMPTS TO
GET CLEAN. I DIDN'T EXPECT THIS ONE TO BE ANY DIFFERENT. I FEARED I WOULD
GO BACK TO THE FAMILIAR, BUT UNHEALTHY RELATIONSHIPS I WAS IN FOR SO MANY YEARS.
I FEARED I WOULD HAVE NO WAY TO SUPPORT MY THREE KIDS ON MY OWN
SINCE I HADN'T WORKED IN YEARS. I HAD SO MUCH FEAR. I KNEW I NEEDED TO
HAVE MORE FAITH, AND THE STEPS HELPED ME TO FIND THAT FAITH."

KRISTINE, IN RECOVERY FOR ELEVEN YEARS

Today's Date _____   Days in Recovery _____

I am *happy* today because _____

_____

_____

_____

_____

I am *able* to_____

_____

_____

_____

_____

_____

_____

_____

_____

_____

Today I learned	Today I did something positive for my recovery by
_____	_____
_____	_____
_____	_____
_____	_____
_____	_____

Today's Date _____   Days in Recovery _____

Today I am *working* on_____

_____

_____

_____

_____

I am moving *forward* with _____

_____

_____

_____

_____

_____

_____

_____

_____

_____

_____

_____

_____

_____

_____

"LET NO ONE SAY THAT TAKING ACTION IS HARD.
ACTION IS AIDED BY COURAGE, BY THE MOMENT, BY IMPULSE,
AND THE HARDEST THING IN THE WORLD IS MAKING A DECISION."
FRANZ GRILLPARZER (1791–1872)

Today's Date _____ Days in Recovery _____

The step I am currently writing on helps me to define *fear* as _____

_____

_____

_____

_____

I *cope* with my fears by _____

_____

_____

_____

_____

_____

_____

_____

_____

_____

_____

_____

_____

_____

"THE THING I FEAR MOST IS FEAR."

MICHEL DE MONTAIGNE (1533–1592)

Today's Date _____   Days in Recovery_____

I believe all of my *needs* are met today because _____

_____

_____

_____

_____

I am living *"just for today"* by _____

_____

_____

_____

_____

_____

_____

_____

_____

_____

_____

_____

_____

_____

"DO NOT SPOIL WHAT YOU HAVE BY DESIRING WHAT YOU HAVE NOT; BUT REMEMBER THAT
WHAT YOU NOW HAVE WAS ONCE AMONG THE THINGS YOU ONLY HOPED FOR."
EPICURUS (341–270 BC)

Today's Date _____   Days in Recovery _____

Right now, I understand *powerlessness* to mean _____

_____

_____

_____

_____

Now that I am in recovery, my *favorite* thing to do is _____

_____

_____

_____

_____

_____

_____

_____

_____

_____

_____

_____

_____

_____

_____

"WE ARE WHAT WE REPEATEDLY DO.
EXCELLENCE, THEREFORE, IS NOT AN ACT BUT A HABIT."
ARISTOTLE (384–322 BC)

Today's Date _____   Days in Recovery _____

My *favorite* people I have met since coming into recovery are_____

_____

_____

_____

_____

Today I understand *friendship* to mean _____

_____

_____

_____

_____

_____

_____

_____

_____

_____

_____

_____

_____

_____

_____

"A MAN'S GROWTH IS SEEN IN HIS SUCCESSIVE CHOIRS OF FRIENDS."
RALPH WALDO EMERSON (1803–1882)

Today's Date _____   Days in Recovery _____

Today I *accomplished* _____

_____

_____

_____

_____

I feel most *connected* to my higher power when _____

_____

_____

_____

_____

_____

_____

_____

Today I learned | Today I did something positive for my recovery by

_____ | _____

_____ | _____

_____ | _____

_____ | _____

_____ | _____

Today's Date _____   Days in Recovery _____

The *recovery-oriented* activities I did today were _____

_____

_____

_____

_____

When I am afraid of *relapse*, I _____

_____

_____

_____

_____

_____

_____

_____

_____

_____

_____

_____

_____

_____

_____

"THE RECOVERY PROCESS REQUIRES THAT ONE DOES SOME BASIC REQUIREMENTS ON A CONSISTENT BASIS SUCH AS NOT USING, ATTENDING MEETINGS, AND CALLING A SPONSOR."

RECOVERY A TO Z: A HANDBOOK OF TWELVE-STEP KEY TERMS AND PHRASES

Today's Date _____   Days in Recovery _____

By staying in recovery I am *choosing* _____

_____

_____

_____

_____

To me, *honesty* is _____

_____

_____

_____

_____

_____

_____

_____

_____

_____

_____

_____

_____

_____

_____

❖❖❖

"TRUTH IS IN THINGS, AND NOT IN WORDS."

HERMAN MELVILLE (1819–1891)

Today's Date _____ Days in Recovery _____

When I think of my new *life* in recovery today, I feel _____

_____

_____

_____

_____

Today when I am *angry*, I _____

_____

_____

_____

_____

_____

_____

_____

_____

_____

_____

_____

_____

_____

"LOSE YOUR TEMPER AND YOU LOSE A FRIEND; LIE AND YOU LOSE YOURSELF."
HOPI SAYING

Today's Date _____   Days in Recovery _____

I define *friendship* as _____

_____

_____

_____

_____

The *friends* I have gained in recovery are _____

_____

_____

_____

_____

_____

_____

_____

_____

_____

_____

_____

_____

_____

_____

"BE COURTEOUS TO ALL, BUT INTIMATE WITH FEW, AND LET THOSE FEW
BE WELL TRIED BEFORE YOU GIVE THEM YOUR CONFIDENCE."
GEORGE WASHINGTON (1732–1799)

Today's Date _____ Days in Recovery _____

Today I am learning to find *strength* and *support* in/with _____

_____

_____

_____

_____

Today I was of *service* to_____

_____

_____

_____

_____

_____

_____

_____

_____

_____

_____

_____

"I LEANED ON FRIENDS IN THE PROGRAM WHO HAD MORE TIME THAN ME.
I COULD SEE THEIR LIVES WERE GOING WELL AND BELIEVED THAT
IF THE PROGRAM WORKED FOR THEM, THEN IT COULD WORK FOR ME, TOO.
MY FAMILY GAVE ME A LOT OF STRENGTH. THE LOVE AND SUPPORT THEY GAVE ME
IN THOSE HARD TIMES WERE REMARKABLE. I ALSO RELIED A LOT ON MY SPONSOR
AND GRAND SPONSOR. I STUCK TO THEM LIKE 'WHITE ON RICE.'"

TRAVIS, IN RECOVERY FOR SIX YEARS

Today's Date _____   Days in Recovery _____

Today I *focused* on _____

_____

_____

_____

_____

When I feel *guilty* or *ashamed* of things I did while I was using, I handle this by _____

_____

_____

_____

_____

_____

_____

_____

_____

Today I learned	Today I did something positive for my recovery by
_____	_____
_____	_____
_____	_____
_____	_____

Today's Date _____   Days in Recovery _____

Today I am learning to be in the *process* of recovery by _____

_____

_____

_____

_____

I am *grateful* for _____

_____

_____

_____

_____

_____

_____

_____

_____

_____

_____

_____

_____

_____

"GOING SLOWLY DOES NOT STOP ONE FROM ARRIVING."
WEST AFRICAN SAYING

Today's Date _____   Days in Recovery _____

Today I understand *surrender* to mean _____

_____

_____

_____

_____

To keep moving *forward* in my recovery, I need _____

_____

_____

_____

_____

_____

_____

_____

_____

_____

_____

_____

_____

"THERE'S A VICTORY AND DEFEAT—THE FIRST AND BEST OF VICTORIES,
THE LOWEST AND WORST OF DEFEATS—WHICH EACH MAN GAINS OR SUSTAINS
AT THE HANDS NOT OF ANOTHER, BUT OF HIMSELF."
PLATO (427–347 BC)

Today's Date _____   Days in Recovery _____

When I listen in meetings, I *hear* _____

_____

_____

_____

_____

To me, *trust is*_____

_____

_____

_____

_____

_____

_____

_____

_____

_____

_____

_____

_____

_____

"IT TAKES TWO TO SPEAK THE TRUTH—ONE TO SPEAK AND ANOTHER TO HEAR."
HENRY DAVID THOREAU (1817–1862)

Today's Date _____   Days in Recovery _____

Some of the *recovery-oriented* activities I did today include _____

_____

_____

_____

_____

The step I am currently writing on is *teaching* me _____

_____

_____

_____

_____

_____

_____

_____

_____

_____

_____

_____

_____

_____

"YOU WILL NEVER PLOUGH A FIELD IF YOU ONLY TURN IT OVER IN YOUR MIND."
IRISH PROVERB

Today's Date _____ Days in Recovery _____

Today when I start to *obsess* about something, I _____

_____

_____

_____

_____

The hardest thing about speaking my *truth* is _____

_____

_____

_____

_____

_____

_____

_____

_____

_____

_____

_____

_____

"WHEN I FOUND MYSELF OBSESSING, I REMINDED MYSELF
'DON'T USE NO MATTER WHAT.' I PRAYED. I CALLED MY SPONSOR."
MEL, IN RECOVERY FOR TWENTY-FIVE YEARS

Today's Date _____   Days in Recovery_____

So far my favorite spiritual *principle* is _____

_____

_____

_____

_____

The reason this is my favorite spiritual *principle* is because_____

_____

_____

_____

_____

_____

_____

_____

_____

Today I learned	Today I did something positive for my recovery by
_____	_____
_____	_____
_____	_____
_____	_____
_____	_____

Today's Date _____   Days in Recovery _____

Today my higher power *offers* me _____

_____

_____

_____

_____

When I think about my *shortcomings*, I _____

_____

_____

_____

_____

_____

_____

_____

_____

_____

_____

_____

_____

_____

"SWEET ARE THE USES OF ADVERSITY
WHICH, LIKE THE TOAD, UGLY AND VENOMOUS,
WEARS YET A PRECIOUS JEWEL IN HIS HEAD."
WILLIAM SHAKESPEARE (1564–1616)

Today's Date _____   Days in Recovery _____

Today I am *capable* of _____

_____

_____

_____

When I face *challenges* I can_____

_____

_____

_____

_____

_____

_____

_____

_____

_____

_____

_____

_____

_____

"IF WE ALL DID THE THINGS WE ARE CAPABLE OF,
WE WOULD ASTOUND OURSELVES."

THOMAS EDISON (1847–1931)

Today's Date _____ Days in Recovery _____

Today I know I can stay in recovery if I _____

_____

_____

_____

_____

I am confident in my *ability* to _____

_____

_____

_____

_____

_____

_____

_____

_____

_____

_____

_____

_____

_____

_____

"BALANCED THINKING RESULTS IN CREATING A REALISTIC SET OF GOALS AND
FOCUSING ENERGY AND EFFORT INTO MAKING PROGRESS TOWARD ACHIEVING EACH ONE."
PAIN RECOVERY: HOW TO FIND BALANCE AND REDUCE SUFFERING FROM CHRONIC PAIN

Today's Date _____   Days in Recovery _____

Today I am facing *challenges* by _____

_____

_____

_____

_____

The step I am currently writing on is helping to *clarify* _____

_____

_____

_____

_____

_____

_____

_____

_____

_____

_____

_____

_____

_____

"PASSION IS POWER,
AND, KINDLY TEMPERED, SAVES. ALL THINGS DECLARE
STRUGGLE HATH DEEPER PEACE THAN SLEEP CAN BRING."
WILLIAM VAUGHN MOODY (1869–1910)

Today's Date _____   Days in Recovery_____

To me, *peace* means _____

_____

_____

_____

_____

I bring *peace* into my life by _____

_____

_____

_____

_____

_____

_____

_____

_____

_____

_____

_____

"NOTHING CAN BRING YOU PEACE BUT YOURSELF."
RALPH WALDO EMERSON (1803–1882)

Today's Date _____   Days in Recovery _____

I *want* _____

_____

_____

_____

_____

When I think about my *willingness* to stay in recovery, I realize _____

_____

_____

_____

_____

_____

_____

_____

_____

Today I learned	Today I did something positive for my recovery by
_____	_____
_____	_____
_____	_____
_____	_____

Today's Date _____   Days in Recovery _____

To me, *awareness* means _____

_____

_____

_____

_____

Recovery has made me more *aware* of _____

_____

_____

_____

_____

_____

_____

_____

_____

_____

_____

_____

_____

_____

_____

"THERE ARE MOMENTS OF EXISTENCE WHEN TIME AND SPACE ARE MORE PROFOUND,
AND THE AWARENESS OF EXISTENCE IS IMMENSELY HEIGHTENED."
CHARLES BAUDELAIRE (1821–1867)

Today's Date _____   Days in Recovery _____

I am learning to *live "just for today"* by _____

_____

_____

_____

_____

By staying in recovery, I am *learning* to_____

_____

_____

_____

_____

_____

_____

_____

_____

_____

_____

_____

_____

_____

"MY FIRST YEAR OF RECOVERY WAS A STRANGE AND MAGICAL TIME. THERE WERE
SO MANY NEW THINGS, THOUGHTS, AND IDEAS. FOR ME, I THINK THE BIGGEST
THING WAS THE REALIZATION THAT I DIDN'T HAVE TO USE, NO MATTER WHAT."

FRANK, IN RECOVERY FOR TWENTY-TWO YEARS

Today's Date _____ Days in Recovery _____

The *changes* I see in myself since getting into recovery include _____

_____

_____

_____

_____

New *activities* I enjoy include _____

_____

_____

_____

_____

_____

_____

_____

_____

_____

_____

_____

_____

"HUMAN BEINGS, BY CHANGING THE INNER ATTITUDES OF THEIR MINDS,
CAN CHANGE THE OUTER ASPECTS OF THEIR LIVES."
WILLIAM JAMES (1842–1910)

Today's Date _____   Days in Recovery _____

I *feel* _____

_____

_____

_____

_____

I recognize that my *character defects* _____

_____

_____

_____

_____

_____

_____

_____

_____

_____

_____

_____

_____

"TO HAVE FAULTS AND NOT TO REFORM THEM—THIS, INDEED,
SHOULD BE PRONOUNCED HAVING FAULTS."
CONFUCIUS (551–479 BC)

Today's Date _____   Days in Recovery _____

When I think about letting go of my *character defects*, I feel _____

_____

_____

_____

_____

Today, *character* means to me _____

_____

_____

_____

_____

_____

_____

_____

_____

_____

_____

_____

_____

_____

"MEN SHOW THEIR CHARACTERS IN NOTHING MORE CLEARLY
THAN IN WHAT THEY THINK LAUGHABLE."

JOHANN WOLFGANG VON GOETHE (1749–1832)

Today's Date _____   Days in Recovery _____

Some of the *changes* I see in my life now are _____

_____

_____

_____

_____

Right now, I *describe* myself as _____

_____

_____

_____

_____

_____

_____

_____

_____

_____

Today I learned	Today I did something positive for my recovery by

Today's Date _____   Days in Recovery _____

Today I understand *obsession* to mean _____

_____

_____

_____

_____

If I find myself *obsessing,* I _____

_____

_____

_____

_____

_____

_____

_____

_____

_____

_____

_____

_____

_____

"WHEN SINS ARE DEAR TO US WE ARE TOO PRONE TO SLIDE INTO THEM AGAIN.
THE ACT OF REPENTANCE ITSELF IS OFTEN SWEETENED WITH THE THOUGHT
THAT IT CLEARS OUR ACCOUNT FOR A REPETITION OF THE SAME SIN."
THOMAS JEFFERSON, (1743–1826)

Today's Date _____ Days in Recovery_____

By staying in recovery, my *self-respect* has _____

_____

_____

_____

Today I am *grateful* for _____

_____

_____

_____

_____

_____

_____

_____

_____

_____

_____

_____

_____

_____

"NEVER ESTEEM ANYTHING AS OF ADVANTAGE TO YOU THAT WILL MAKE YOU
BREAK YOUR WORD OR LOSE YOUR SELF-RESPECT."
MARCUS AURELIUS ANTONINUS (121–180)

Today's Date _____   Days in Recovery _____

I understand the word *humility* to mean _____

_____

_____

_____

_____

I am learning *humility* from _____

_____

_____

_____

_____

_____

_____

_____

_____

_____

_____

_____

_____

"HUMILITY DOES NOT MEAN THINKING LESS OF YOURSELF THAN OF OTHER PEOPLE,
NOR DOES IT MEAN HAVING A LOW OPINION OF YOUR OWN GIFTS.
IT MEANS FREEDOM FROM THINKING ABOUT YOURSELF AT ALL."
WILLIAM TEMPLE (1628–1699)

Today's Date _____   Days in Recovery _____

I feel *happy* right now because_____

_____

_____

_____

_____

I keep my *sense of humor* by _____

_____

_____

_____

_____

_____

_____

_____

_____

_____

_____

_____

_____

_____

"HAPPINESS DEPENDS MORE ON THE INWARD DISPOSITION OF THE MIND
THAN ON OUTWARD CIRCUMSTANCES."
BENJAMIN FRANKLIN (1706–1790)

Today's Date _____   Days in Recovery _____

Today I felt *angry* when _____

_____

_____

_____

_____

I addressed my *anger* by _____

_____

_____

_____

_____

_____

_____

_____

_____

_____

_____

_____

_____

"HOLDING ONTO ANGER IS LIKE GRASPING A HOT COAL
WITH THE INTENT OF THROWING IT AT SOMEONE ELSE;
YOU ARE ALWAYS THE ONE WHO GETS BURNED."
SIDDHARTHA GAUTAMA BUDDHA (563–483 BC)

Today's Date _____ Days in Recovery _____

Since getting into recovery I have _____

_____

_____

_____

_____

My life is *changing* by _____

_____

_____

_____

_____

_____

_____

_____

_____

Today I learned	Today I did something positive for my recovery by
_____	_____
_____	_____
_____	_____
_____	_____
_____	_____

Today's Date _____   Days in Recovery _____

From the step I am currently writing on, I am *learning* _____

_____

_____

_____

_____

I like *learning* this because _____

_____

_____

_____

_____

_____

_____

_____

_____

_____

_____

_____

_____

_____

"NOTHING EVER IS, BUT ALL THINGS ARE BECOMING...
ALL THINGS ARE THE OFFSPRING OF FLUX AND MOTION."
SOCRATES (470–399 BC)

Today's Date _____   Days in Recovery _____

Change has been easy for me because _____

_____

_____

_____

_____

Change has been difficult for me because _____

_____

_____

_____

_____

_____

_____

_____

_____

_____

_____

_____

_____

"WHEN YOU MAKE A MISTAKE, DON'T LOOK BACK AT IT LONG.
TAKE THE REASON OF THE THING INTO YOUR MIND AND THEN LOOK FORWARD.
MISTAKES ARE LESSONS OF WISDOM. THE PAST CANNOT BE CHANGED.
THE FUTURE IS YET IN YOUR POWER."

HUGH WHITE (1773–1840)

Today's Date _____   Days in Recovery_____

When I *wake* up in the morning, I usually will _____

_____

_____

_____

_____

I *quiet* my mind by _____

_____

_____

_____

_____

_____

_____

_____

_____

_____

_____

_____

"YOU DO NOT NEED TO LEAVE YOUR ROOM. REMAIN SITTING AT YOUR TABLE AND LISTEN.
DO NOT EVEN LISTEN, SIMPLY WAIT, BE QUIET, STILL, AND SOLITARY. THE WORLD
WILL FREELY OFFER ITSELF TO YOU TO BE UNMASKED, IT HAS NO CHOICE;
IT WILL ROLL IN ECSTASY AT YOUR FEET."

FRANZ KAFKA (1883–1924)

Today's Date _____   Days in Recovery _____

Today *inspiration* means to me _____

_____

_____

_____

_____

I am most *inspired* by _____

_____

_____

_____

_____

_____

_____

_____

_____

_____

_____

_____

_____

_____

"GO CONFIDENTLY IN THE DIRECTION OF YOUR DREAMS.
LIVE THE LIFE YOU HAVE IMAGINED."
HENRY DAVID THOREAU (1817–1862)

Today's Date _____   Days in Recovery _____

Today, *amending* my behavior means that I _____

_____

_____

_____

_____

When I think of *amends,* I feel _____

_____

_____

_____

_____

_____

_____

_____

_____

_____

_____

_____

_____

_____

"RESOLVE, AND THOU ARE FREE."
HENRY WADSWORTH LONGFELLOW (1807–1882)

Today's Date _____   Days in Recovery _____

The step I am currently writing on is *teaching* me _____

_____

_____

_____

_____

I am *determined* to _____

_____

_____

_____

_____

_____

_____

_____

_____

Today I learned	Today I did something positive for my recovery by
_____	_____
_____	_____
_____	_____
_____	_____

Today's Date _____   Days in Recovery _____

Today I *understand* _____

_____

_____

_____

_____

I still struggle to *understand*_____

_____

_____

_____

_____

_____

_____

_____

_____

_____

_____

_____

_____

_____

"WHAT ONE DOESN'T UNDERSTAND ONE DOESN'T POSSESS."
JOHANN WOLFGANG VON GOETHE (1749–1832)

Today's Date _____   Days in Recovery _____

Right now, *forgiveness* means _____

_____

_____

_____

_____

When I think about *forgiveness,* I _____

_____

_____

_____

_____

_____

_____

_____

_____

_____

_____

_____

_____

_____

_____

"WE PARDON TO THE EXTENT THAT WE LOVE."

FRANÇOIS VI, DUC DE LA ROCHEFOUCAULD, LE PRINCE DE MARCILLAC (1613–1680)

Today's Date _____   Days in Recovery _____

I am *grateful* for _____

_____

_____

_____

_____

When I dream of my *future*, I feel _____

_____

_____

_____

_____

_____

_____

_____

_____

_____

_____

_____

_____

_____

_____

"A DREAM IS A PROPHECY IN MINIATURE."

TALMUD, BERAKOT 55A

Today's Date _____   Days in Recovery _____

I *hope* _____

_____

_____

_____

_____

To ensure I stay in *recovery,* I need to _____

_____

_____

_____

_____

_____

_____

_____

_____

_____

_____

_____

_____

"IN THE BEGINNING, I WAS DEPRESSED AND ANGRY. I DIDN'T SLEEP
AND I WAS DEFENSIVE. GRADUALLY I LEARNED ABOUT THESE AS
COMPONENTS OF MY DISEASE AND WORKED TOWARD RECOVERY. I GOT RELIEF
FROM MY SYMPTOMS BY WORKING THE STEPS AND GOING TO MEETINGS."

MEL, IN RECOVERY FOR TWENTY-FIVE YEARS

Today's Date _____   Days in Recovery _____

I am *accountable* today because _____

_____

_____

_____

_____

The people I *count* on are _____

_____

_____

_____

_____

_____

_____

_____

_____

_____

_____

_____

_____

"WE JUDGE OURSELVES BY WHAT WE FEEL CAPABLE OF DOING,
WHILE OTHERS JUDGE US BY WHAT WE HAVE ALREADY DONE."
HENRY WADSWORTH LONGFELLOW (1807–1882)

Today's Date _____   Days in Recovery _____

Today I *learned* these things about myself _____

_____

_____

_____

_____

At the most recent meeting I attended, I *learned* _____

_____

_____

_____

_____

_____

_____

_____

_____

Today I learned	Today I did something positive for my recovery by
_____	_____
_____	_____
_____	_____
_____	_____

Today's Date _____ Days in Recovery _____

Today I understand *fear* to mean _____

_____

_____

_____

_____

My sponsor gives me the *courage* to _____

_____

_____

_____

_____

_____

_____

_____

_____

_____

_____

_____

_____

"COURAGE IS RESISTANCE TO FEAR, MASTERY OF FEAR—NOT ABSENCE OF FEAR."
MARK TWAIN (1835–1910)

Today's Date _____   Days in Recovery _____

The things I *value* in my life today are _____

_____

_____

_____

_____

The people I *value* in my life today include _____

_____

_____

_____

_____

_____

_____

_____

_____

_____

_____

_____

_____

_____

"THAT WHICH COSTS LITTLE IS LESS VALUED."

MIGUEL DE CERVANTES (1547–1616)

Today's Date _____   Days in Recovery _____

The step I am currently writing on is *teaching* me _____

_____

_____

_____

_____

I am *able* to _____

_____

_____

_____

_____

_____

_____

_____

_____

_____

_____

_____

_____

_____

_____

_____

"HEAVEN SUITS THE BACK TO THE BURDEN."
CHARLES DICKENS (1812–1870)

Today's Date _____   Days in Recovery _____

Since getting into recovery, I have made the following *changes* _____

_____

_____

_____

_____

Change makes me feel_____

_____

_____

_____

_____

_____

_____

_____

_____

_____

_____

_____

_____

_____

"NOTHING ENDURES BUT CHANGE."
HERACLITUS (535–475 BC)

Today's Date _____   Days in Recovery _____

I *surround* myself with people who _____

_____

_____

_____

_____

I stay healthy by *avoiding* people who_____

_____

_____

_____

_____

_____

_____

_____

_____

_____

_____

_____

_____

_____

_____

"NOTHING IS AT LAST SACRED BUT THE INTEGRITY OF YOUR OWN MIND."
RALPH WALDO EMERSON (1803–1882)

Today's Date _____   Days in Recovery_____

Today I understand *spiritual* principles to mean _____

_____

_____

_____

Some of my favorite spiritual *principles* are _____

_____

_____

_____

_____

_____

_____

_____

Today I learned	Today I did something positive for my recovery by
_____	_____
_____	_____
_____	_____
_____	_____

Today's Date _____   Days in Recovery _____

Today I understand *sincerity* to mean _____

_____

_____

_____

_____

I am *sincere* in my efforts to _____

_____

_____

_____

_____

_____

_____

_____

_____

_____

_____

_____

_____

"WHEN THE WILL IS SINCERE, THEN THE HEART IS SET RIGHT."
CONFUCIUS (551–479 BC)

Today's Date _____   Days in Recovery _____

My understanding of *acceptance* has _____

_____

_____

_____

_____

Today I find myself more *willing* to _____

_____

_____

_____

_____

_____

_____

_____

_____

_____

_____

_____

_____

_____

_____

_____

"LIFE WITHOUT ENDEAVOR IS LIKE ENTERING A JEWEL MINE
AND COMING OUT WITH EMPTY HANDS."

JAPANESE PROVERB

Today's Date _____   Days in Recovery _____

Being in recovery helps me to stay in the *present* by _____

_____

_____

_____

_____

Today I understand *"making plans"* to mean _____

_____

_____

_____

_____

_____

_____

_____

_____

_____

_____

_____

_____

_____

_____

"I KNOW YOU HATE IT WHEN I SAY THIS, BUT I WANT YOU
TO PRACTICE BEING A VERY SIMPLE, HUMBLE PERSON."
SYDNEY (1925–2005), IN RECOVERY FOR THIRTY YEARS

Today's Date _____   Days in Recovery _____

When I feel like *giving* up, I _____

_____

_____

_____

_____

My recovery is *important* to me today because _____

_____

_____

_____

_____

_____

_____

_____

_____

_____

_____

_____

_____

_____

"WE PROMISE ACCORDING TO OUR HOPES
AND PERFORM ACCORDING TO OUR FEARS."
FRANÇOIS DE LA ROCHEFOUCAULD (1613–1680)

Today's Date _____   Days in Recovery _____

Today I can *look* in the mirror and say _____

_____

_____

_____

_____

I like where I am going in *recovery* because _____

_____

_____

_____

_____

_____

_____

_____

_____

_____

_____

_____

_____

"I FIND THE GREAT THING IN THIS WORLD IS NOT SO MUCH WHERE WE STAND,
AS IN WHAT DIRECTION WE ARE MOVING."
OLIVER WENDELL HOLMES (1809–1894)

Today's Date _____   Days in Recovery _____

Today my *dreams* include _____

_____

_____

_____

_____

My *goals* for today include _____

_____

_____

_____

_____

_____

_____

_____

_____

Today I learned	Today I did something positive for my recovery by
_____	_____
_____	_____
_____	_____
_____	_____
_____	_____

Today's Date _____   Days in Recovery _____

Today I *understand* these things about myself _____

_____

_____

_____

_____

I work toward *self-awareness* by _____

_____

_____

_____

_____

_____

_____

_____

_____

_____

_____

_____

_____

_____

"HE WHO KNOWS OTHERS IS CLEVER;
HE WHO KNOWS HIMSELF HAS DISCERNMENT."
LAO-TZU (604–531 BC)

Today's Date _____   Days in Recovery _____

My biggest *assets* are _____

_____

_____

_____

_____

Some of the things I like about *myself* today are _____

_____

_____

_____

_____

_____

_____

_____

_____

_____

_____

_____

_____

❖⟞⟑⟨⟩⟑⟞❖

"AS I BECOME MORE MINDFUL OF THE MANY BLESSINGS IN MY LIFE AND LEARN HOW TO
MAINTAIN CONSCIOUS CONTACT WITH MY GRATITUDE FOR THEM, MY SPIRITUALITY DEEPENS,
MY RECOVERY GETS STRONGER, AND I TAKE A FEW MORE STEPS TOWARD GRACE."

TAILS OF RECOVERY: ADDICTS AND THE PETS THAT LOVE THEM

Today's Date _____ Days in Recovery_____

Today I *understand* shortcomings to mean _____

_____

_____

_____

_____

The *shortcomings* I am working on are_____

_____

_____

_____

_____

_____

_____

_____

_____

_____

_____

_____

_____

_____

_____

"THE SECRET OF HEALTH FOR BOTH MIND AND BODY IS NOT TO MOURN FOR THE PAST,
NOT TO WORRY ABOUT THE FUTURE, OR NOT TO ANTICIPATE TROUBLES,
BUT TO LIVE THE PRESENT MOMENT WISELY AND EARNESTLY."
SIDDHARTHA GAUTAMA BUDDHA (563–483 BC)

Today's Date _____   Days in Recovery _____

The step I am currently writing on is *teaching* me _____

_____

_____

_____

_____

I believe my *experiences* are _____

_____

_____

_____

_____

_____

_____

_____

_____

_____

_____

_____

_____

_____

"EXPERIENCE IS THE NAME EVERYONE GIVES TO THEIR MISTAKES."
OSCAR WILDE (1854–1900)

Today's Date _____ Days in Recovery_____

Sharing my *experiences* with my sponsor is _____

_____

_____

_____

_____

When I am *honestly* sharing with my sponsor, I feel _____

_____

_____

_____

_____

_____

_____

_____

_____

_____

_____

_____

_____

_____

"MY HOPE WAS THAT I COULD LIVE A CLEAN LIFE
AND TODAY THAT HOPE IS A REALITY."
BOBBY, (1934-2008) IN RECOVERY FOR THIRTY-FOUR YEARS

Today's Date _____   Days in Recovery _____

"Just for today" I will _____

_____

_____

_____

I *want* _____

_____

_____

_____

_____

_____

_____

Today I learned

_____

_____

_____

_____

Today I did something positive for my recovery by

_____

_____

_____

_____

Today's Date _____   Days in Recovery_____

To me, *self-knowledge* means_____

_____

_____

_____

_____

I am striving for *self-knowledge* by_____

_____

_____

_____

_____

_____

_____

_____

_____

_____

_____

_____

_____

_____

"RESOLVE TO BE THYSELF, AND KNOW THAT
HE WHO FINDS HIMSELF, LOSES HIS MISERY."
MATTHEW ARNOLD (1822–1888)

Today's Date _____ Days in Recovery _____

Today I understand *control* to mean _____

_____

_____

_____

_____

Today I understand *self-control* to mean _____

_____

_____

_____

_____

_____

_____

_____

_____

_____

_____

_____

_____

"A LITTLE KINGDOM I POSSESS,
WHERE THOUGHTS AND FEELINGS DWELL.
AND VERY HARD THE TASK I FIND
OF GOVERNING IT WELL."
LOUISA MAY ALCOTT (1832–1888)

Today's Date _____   Days in Recovery _____

Since coming into recovery, I *love* to _____

_____

_____

_____

_____

Today I *enjoy* _____

_____

_____

_____

_____

_____

_____

_____

_____

_____

_____

_____

_____

_____

"IT IS NOT DOING THE THING WE LIKE TO DO,
BUT LIKING THE THING WE HAVE TO DO, THAT MAKES LIFE BLESSED."
JOHANN WOLFGANG VON GOETHE (1749–1832)

Today's Date _____   Days in Recovery _____

Today I find *strength* in _____

_____

_____

_____

_____

Today my higher power *helps* me to _____

_____

_____

_____

_____

_____

_____

_____

_____

_____

_____

_____

_____

_____

_____

"FOR STRENGTH, I LEAN ON MY SPONSOR, OTHER RECOVERING ADDICTS, AND
A LOVING GOD THAT I KNOW LOVES ME, EVEN WHEN I DON'T FEEL LOVE AT ALL."

BILL, IN RECOVERY FOR SEVEN YEARS

Today's Date _____   Days in Recovery _____

Today I define *spirituality* as _____

_____

_____

_____

_____

To connect with my *spirituality*, I _____

_____

_____

_____

_____

_____

_____

_____

_____

_____

_____

_____

_____

_____

_____

"THE MOST SPIRITUAL HUMAN BEINGS, ASSUMING THEY ARE THE MOST COURAGEOUS,
ALSO EXPERIENCE BY FAR THE MOST PAINFUL TRAGEDIES:
BUT IT IS PRECISELY FOR THIS REASON THAT THEY HONOR LIFE,
BECAUSE IT BRINGS AGAINST THEM ITS MOST FORMIDABLE WEAPONS."
FRIEDRICH NIETZSCHE (1844–1900)

Today's Date _____   Days in Recovery _____

Today I _____

_____

_____

_____

_____

When I *meditate* or *pray,* I feel _____

_____

_____

_____

_____

_____

_____

_____

Today I learned	Today I did something positive for my recovery by

Today's Date _____   Days in Recovery _____

Today I *tried* _____

_____

_____

_____

_____

Today I understand *action* to mean _____

_____

_____

_____

_____

_____

_____

_____

_____

_____

_____

_____

_____

_____

"A PROMISE IS A CLOUD; FULFILLMENT IS RAIN."
ARABIAN PROVERB

Today's Date _____   Days in Recovery _____

When I *talk* with or *pray* to my higher power, I _____

_____

_____

_____

_____

Taking a daily *inventory* is teaching me _____

_____

_____

_____

_____

_____

_____

_____

_____

_____

_____

_____

_____

_____

_____

_____

"THERE ARE THOUGHTS WHICH ARE PRAYERS. THERE ARE MOMENTS WHEN,
WHATEVER THE POSTURE OF THE BODY, THE SOUL IS ON ITS KNEES."
VICTOR HUGO (1802–1885)

Today's Date _____ Days in Recovery _____

The last time I *cried* was _____

_____

_____

_____

_____

The *funniest* thing that happened today was _____

_____

_____

_____

_____

_____

_____

_____

_____

_____

_____

_____

_____

_____

"ACCEPTING YOUR FEELINGS TAKES LESS ENERGY
THAN TRYING TO DENY OR SUPPRESS THEM."
PAIN RECOVERY: HOW TO FIND BALANCE AND REDUCE SUFFERING FROM CHRONIC PAIN

Today's Date _____   Days in Recovery _____

I feel challenged by the step I am currently *writing* on because _____

_____

_____

_____

_____

My sponsor is helping me meet this *challenge* by _____

_____

_____

_____

_____

_____

_____

_____

_____

_____

_____

_____

_____

_____

"TO WITHDRAW MYSELF FROM MYSELF...HAS EVER BEEN MY SOLE,
MY ENTIRE, MY SINCERE MOTIVE IN SCRIBING AT ALL."
LORD BYRON (1788–1824)

Today's Date _____   Days in Recovery _____

Today my sponsor helped me to *understand* _____

_____

_____

_____

_____

I am *learning* to _____

_____

_____

_____

_____

_____

_____

_____

_____

_____

_____

_____

_____

_____

"SOME MEN GO THROUGH A FOREST AND SEE NO FIREWOOD."
ENGLISH PROVERB

Today's Date _____   Days in Recovery _____

Today I describe my *recovery* as _____

_____

_____

_____

_____

My sponsor helps me to be more *aware* of _____

_____

_____

_____

_____

_____

_____

_____

_____

_____

Today I learned	Today I did something positive for my recovery by
_____	_____
_____	_____
_____	_____
_____	_____

Today's Date _____   Days in Recovery _____

Today I am most *honest* with _____

_____

_____

_____

_____

Honesty is important to my recovery because _____

_____

_____

_____

_____

_____

_____

_____

_____

_____

_____

_____

_____

_____

"A TURNING POINT FOR ME WAS OVERCOMING MY DENIAL THAT
I TRULY COULD BE AN ADDICT LIKE 'THE REST OF THEM.'
I HAD TO IDENTIFY WITH OTHERS IN THE MEETINGS."

MEL, IN RECOVERY FOR TWENTY-FIVE YEARS

Today's Date _____   Days in Recovery _____

Today I *reached out* to _____

_____

_____

_____

_____

Today I am not *afraid* to _____

_____

_____

_____

_____

_____

_____

_____

_____

_____

_____

_____

_____

_____

"IN RECOVERY, ISOLATION, WHETHER DELIBERATE OR UNINTENTIONAL,
OFTEN PRECEDES A RELAPSE."
RECOVERY A TO Z: A HANDBOOK OF TWELVE-STEP KEY TERMS AND PHRASES

Today's Date _____   Days in Recovery _____

Today I find *wonder* in _____

_____

_____

_____

_____

I am *amazed* by _____

_____

_____

_____

_____

_____

_____

_____

_____

_____

_____

_____

_____

_____

"WONDER IS THE FEELING OF THE PHILOSOPHER,
AND PHILOSOPHY BEGINS IN WONDER."
PLATO (427–347 BC)

Today's Date _____   Days in Recovery _____

My favorite principles I *learned* about today are _____

_____

_____

_____

_____

The step I am currently writing on is *teaching* me _____

_____

_____

_____

_____

_____

_____

_____

_____

_____

_____

_____

_____

"THE SURE CONVICTION THAT WE COULD IF WE WANTED TO
IS THE REASON SO MANY GOOD MINDS ARE IDLE."
G. C. LICHTENBERG (1742–1799)

Today's Date _____   Days in Recovery _____

Today it is *important* for me to _____

_____

_____

_____

_____

To continue to move forward in my *recovery,* I know I must_____

_____

_____

_____

_____

_____

_____

_____

_____

_____

_____

_____

_____

_____

"HE WHO WAITS TO DO A GREAT DEAL OF GOOD AT ONCE,
WILL NEVER DO ANYTHING."

SAMUEL JOHNSON (1709–1784)

Today's Date _____   Days in Recovery _____

Today I understand "being of *service*" to mean _____

_____

_____

_____

_____

Self-love is important to me because _____

_____

_____

_____

_____

_____

_____

_____

_____

Today I learned	Today I did something positive for my recovery by
_____	_____
_____	_____
_____	_____
_____	_____

Today's Date _____   Days in Recovery _____

Today I describe my *recovery* as _____

_____

_____

_____

_____

Attending *meetings* makes me feel _____

_____

_____

_____

_____

_____

_____

_____

_____

_____

_____

_____

_____

_____

_____

"FOR I HAVE LEARNED, IN WHATSOEVER STATE I AM, THEREWITH TO BE CONTENT."

BIBLE: NEW TESTAMENT, PHILIPPIANS 4:11

Today's Date _____   Days in Recovery_____

Since coming into recovery, I have *changed* in the following ways _____

_____

_____

_____

_____

I *want* to be _____

_____

_____

_____

_____

_____

_____

_____

_____

_____

_____

_____

_____

_____

_____

"FIRST SAY TO YOURSELF WHAT YOU WOULD BE;
AND THEN DO WHAT YOU HAVE TO DO."
EPICTETUS (55–135)

Today's Date _____   Days in Recovery _____

The best *book* I have read since coming into recovery is _____

_____

_____

_____

_____

Some of the things I *learned* from this book include_____

_____

_____

_____

_____

_____

_____

_____

_____

_____

_____

_____

_____

_____

_____

"THAT IS A GOOD BOOK WHICH IS OPENED WITH EXPECTATION
AND CLOSED WITH PROFIT."
A. BRONSON ALCOTT (1799–1888)

Today's Date _____   Days in Recovery _____

My *sponsor* is helping me to understand _____

_____

_____

_____

_____

My *goal* for today is _____

_____

_____

_____

_____

_____

_____

_____

_____

_____

_____

IF I CAN STOP ONE HEART FROM BREAKING, I SHALL NOT LIVE IN VAIN.
IF I CAN EASE ONE LIFE THE ACHING,
OR COOL ONE PAIN,
OR HELP ONE FAINTING ROBIN
UNTO HIS NEST AGAIN,
I SHALL NOT LIVE IN VAIN.

EMILY DICKINSON (1830–1886)

Today's Date _____   Days in Recovery _____

Today I *learned* _____

_____

_____

_____

_____

Learning this has helped me to *understand* _____

_____

_____

_____

_____

_____

_____

_____

_____

_____

_____

_____

_____

_____

"MUCH LEARNING DOES NOT TEACH UNDERSTANDING."
HERACLITUS (535–475 BC)

Today's Date _____ Days in Recovery _____

To me, *friendship* means _____

_____

_____

_____

_____

The friends I am gaining in *recovery* are _____

_____

_____

_____

_____

_____

_____

_____

_____

Today I learned	Today I did something positive for my recovery by
_____	_____
_____	_____
_____	_____
_____	_____

Today's Date _____   Days in Recovery _____

From the principles of my recovery program, I am *learning* _____

_____

_____

_____

_____

Today I have *faith* in _____

_____

_____

_____

_____

_____

_____

_____

_____

_____

_____

_____

_____

_____

❖

"FAITH IS BELIEVING WHAT YOU DO NOT SEE;
THE REWARD OF FAITH IS TO SEE WHAT YOU BELIEVE."
ST. AUGUSTINE (354–430)

Today's Date _____   Days in Recovery_____

The ways in which my *dreams* have changed since coming into recovery are _____

_____

_____

_____

_____

Today I *dream* of _____

_____

_____

_____

_____

_____

_____

_____

_____

_____

_____

_____

_____

_____

"I HAVE DREAMT IN MY LIFE, DREAMS THAT HAVE STAYED WITH ME EVER AFTER,
AND CHANGED MY IDEAS; THEY HAVE GONE THROUGH AND THROUGH ME...
AND ALTERED THE COLOR OF MY MIND."
EMILY BRONTE (1818–1848)

Today's Date _____   Days in Recovery _____

The *step* I am currently writing on is _____

_____

_____

_____

_____

Writing in this *journal* has helped me to _____

_____

_____

_____

_____

_____

_____

_____

_____

_____

_____

_____

_____

"I HAVE NEVER THOUGHT OF WRITING FOR REPUTATION AND HONOR.
WHAT I HAVE IN MY HEART MUST COME OUT; THAT IS THE REASON WHY I COMPOSE."
LUDWIG VAN BEETHOVEN (1770–1827)

Today's Date _____   Days in Recovery _____

Today I am *hopeful* that _____

_____

_____

_____

_____

The step I am currently writing on is *challenging* because _____

_____

_____

_____

_____

_____

_____

_____

_____

_____

_____

_____

_____

_____

"IF YOU WISH SUCCESS IN LIFE, MAKE PERSEVERANCE YOUR BOSOM FRIEND,
EXPERIENCE YOUR WISE COUNSELOR, CAUTION YOUR ELDER BROTHER
AND HOPE YOUR GUARDIAN GENIUS."
JOSEPH ADDISON (1672–1719)

Today's Date _____   Days in Recovery _____

Today is *important* because _____

_____

_____

_____

_____

I *believe* _____

_____

_____

_____

_____

_____

_____

_____

_____

_____

_____

_____

_____

"HOPE IS A WAKING DREAM."

ARISTOTLE (384–322 BC)

Today's Date _____   Days in Recovery _____

Today I *hope* to _____

_____

_____

_____

_____

I *am*_____

_____

_____

_____

_____

_____

_____

_____

_____

Today I learned	Today I did something positive for my recovery by
_____	_____
_____	_____
_____	_____
_____	_____

Today's Date _____ Days in Recovery _____

Today *success* means to me _____

_____

_____

_____

_____

Today I *succeeded* at _____

_____

_____

_____

_____

_____

_____

_____

_____

_____

_____

_____

_____

"DON'T BE DISCOURAGED BY A FAILURE. IT CAN BE A POSITIVE EXPERIENCE.
FAILURE IS, IN A SENSE, THE HIGHWAY TO SUCCESS, INASMUCH AS EVERY DISCOVERY
OF WHAT IS FALSE LEADS US TO SEEK EARNESTLY AFTER WHAT IS TRUE,
AND EVERY FRESH EXPERIENCE POINTS OUT SOME FORM OF ERROR
WHICH WE SHALL AFTERWARDS CAREFULLY AVOID."
JOHN KEATS (1795–1821)

Today's Date _____ Days in Recovery _____

When I think of reaching my *one-year* anniversary, I feel _____

_____

_____

_____

_____

I stay in the *"here and now"* by _____

_____

_____

_____

_____

_____

_____

_____

_____

_____

_____

_____

"I STILL GET OVERWHELMED WHEN I REACH A RECOVERY BIRTHDAY.
I DON'T THINK I'LL EVER LOSE THAT AWE (AT LEAST I HOPE I NEVER LOSE IT!),
BECAUSE STAYING IN RECOVERY GOES AGAINST EVERYTHING IN MY NATURE.
THE DAY I STOP FEELING THAT AWE IS THE DAY I WILL PICK UP.
I FIRMLY BELIEVE IF I USE TODAY, I WILL DIE. TODAY I WANT TO LIVE."

NANCY, IN RECOVERY FOR TWENTY-SEVEN YEARS

Today's Date _____   Days in Recovery _____

I am the most *proud* of _____

_____

_____

_____

_____

Today I *achieved* _____

_____

_____

_____

_____

_____

_____

_____

_____

_____

_____

_____

"IT'S HARD TO DESCRIBE THE FEELINGS I HAD WHEN I PICKED UP MY KEY TAGS.
EACH ONE WAS A BUILDING BLOCK OF SELF-ESTEEM AND ACCOMPLISHMENT.
I CARRIED THOSE KEY TAGS WITH ME ALL THE TIME. WHEN I PICKED UP MY ONE-YEAR
KEY TAG, IT WAS ALMOST SURREAL. MY MIND COULDN'T ACCEPT THE FACT I HADN'T
USED ANYTHING FOR ONE YEAR. IT WAS TRULY A MIRACLE FOR ME. THE ONE-YEAR
KEY TAG GLOWS IN THE DARK, SO I WENT HOME AND KEPT TURNING OFF THE LIGHTS
OVER AND OVER AGAIN. I LOVED WATCHING IT GLOW IN THE DARK!"

FRANK, IN RECOVERY FOR TWENTY-TWO YEARS

"The worst loneliness is not to be comfortable with yourself."

<small>MARK TWAIN (1835-1910)</small>

"Not until we are lost do we begin to understand ourselves."

<small>HENRY DAVID THOREAU (1817-1862)</small>

CITATIONS

Preamble to the Constitution of the World Health Organization as adopted
by the International Health Conference, New York, 19 June–22 July 1946; signed
on 22 July 1946 by the representatives of 61 States (Official Records of the World
Health Organization, no. 2, p. 100) and entered into force on 7 April 1948.
The definition has not been amended since 1948., 13

My Favorite Memories Of

When I received my thirty-day key tag/chip_____

_____

_____

_____

_____

_____

_____

When I received my sixty-day key tag/chip _____

_____

_____

_____

_____

_____

When I received my ninety-day key tag/chip _____

_____

_____

_____

_____

_____

My Favorite Memories Of

When I received my six-month key tag/chip _____

_____

_____

_____

_____

_____

_____

When I received my nine-month key tag/chip _____

_____

_____

_____

_____

_____

When I received my one-year key tag/chip_____

_____

_____

_____

_____

_____

Name _____

Address _____

_____

Email _____

Name _____

Address _____

_____

Email _____

Name _____

Address _____

_____

Email _____

Name _____

Address _____

_____

Email _____

Name _____

Address _____

_____

Email _____

Name _____

Address _____

_____

Email _____

Name _____

Address _____

_____

Email _____

Name _____

Address _____

_____

Email _____

Name _____

Address _____

_____

Email _____

Name _____

Address _____

_____

Email _____

Name _____

Address _____

_____

Email _____

Name _____

Address _____

_____

Email _____

Name _____

Address _____

_____

Email _____

Name _____

Address _____

_____

Email _____

Name _____

Address _____

_____

Email _____

Name _____

Address _____

_____

Email _____

Name _____

Address _____

_____

Email _____

Name _____

Address _____

_____

Email _____

Name _____

Address _____

_____

Email _____

Name _____

Address _____

_____

Email _____